Valentine: the Quintessential Vampire

A play

Peter Brammer

Samuel French — London
www.samuelfrench-london.co.uk

Please see page iv for further copyright information

VALENTINE: THE
QUINTESSENTIAL VAMPIRE

This version of the play was first presented at the Colourhouse Theatre in Merton Abbey Mills on 31st October 2011 with the following cast:

Valentine	Daniel Howard
Natalia	R.J. Seeley
Hayley	Bethan Lee
Vincent	Marco Rossi
Marianne	Lucie Novak

Directed by Peter Brammer
Designed by Peter Brammer
Lighting designed by Christina Nunes
Original artwork by Rachel Pidoux-Smith

CHARACTERS

Valentine, not a typical vampire: a fairly normal, good-looking young man. His complexion is paler than normal.

Natalia, an effortlessly attractive vampire, dark hair, pale skin and always dressed to impress

Hayley, Valentine's love interest, an attractive girl next door. She should be in stark contrast to all the vampires except perhaps Valentine.

Vincent, Valentine's father, an old school vampire and should be dressed as such. Bela Lugosi is a good guide for his look.

Marianne, Valentine's mother, similar to Valentine in that she is not an obvious vampire but is again pale and does wear more black than is normal.

PRODUCTION NOTES

Staging

The original production used a minimal set to create the three main settings — Valentine's kitchen, living room and the flower shop. Tables and chairs served as setting for kitchen and flower shop with relevant props to indicate the different areas (flowers for the florist, tea cups for the kitchen etc.). A sofa was used to represent the living room and a table and chairs for the restaurant.

Any other settings, such as the bathroom, were positioned in the different areas of the stage and represented by lighting the playing area for that scene.

Pace and Cuts

The first act is long, but is to be performed at pace, particularly the scenes with Natalia and Valentine. If, however, the play is found to overrun, the author is open to cuts and has a list of suggestions to reduce the running time. These are available by using the email below.

For more information please email peterbrammerpw@gmail.com

Time — the present

AUTHOR'S NOTE

I would like to thank the following for their
advice and help in developing this project:

Michelene Heine, Samuel Lewis, Sophia Ellis,
Marco Rossi, Daniel Howard, Bethan Lee, Lucie Novak.

The Heather Brothers for their support and
belief in the piece.

A special thank you to my wife Rachel Pidoux-Smith
for all her artwork and support.

My father, Raymond Smith, to whom all my work is
dedicated, whose support and belief in my work
never wavered.

Peter Brammer

ACT I

SCENE 1

Valentine's flat, the kitchen. Night

It is dark. Natalia is sitting in the dark, knitting. She has a bottle of blood concealed on her person. A key can be heard turning in a lock. A door opens and is closed. There are footsteps followed by someone tripping over a large object

Valentine (*off*) What the —— ?

Moments later Valentine enters and switches on the light to reveal Natalia

He takes off his cloak and sits opposite her

Natalia Good-evening.
Valentine What is that in the hallway?
Natalia What is what?
Valentine The thing I almost broke my neck on when I fell over it getting to the kitchen?
Natalia Oh that, that's Frank.
Valentine Frank?
Natalia Frank, Francis, Frankie ... whatever.
Valentine Is he dead?
Natalia Lying motionless on the ground? Yes, I should think so.
Valentine Did you?
Natalia Did I what?
Valentine Did you ... you know? (*He makes a throat-slitting gesture*)
Natalia What on earth is that supposed to be?
Valentine Did you kill him?
Natalia No, I made him supper and sent him on his way and he collapsed in the hallway.
Valentine Thank God ——
Natalia Of course I killed him, he's dead on the floor. I suppose in a way I did make him supper ... my supper.
Valentine Natalia, you've got to stop doing this. People will get suspicious.

Natalia I've been doing this since we moved here. Nobody's got suspicious yet. We chop him up into tiny pieces, put the bits in secure black bin bags, job done and nobody has seen a thing.

Valentine People must see you bringing these people back?

Natalia I'm careful to pick and choose people that won't be missed and usher them into the flat under cover of darkness. Anyway I'm not sure anyone would care. I swear the old lady upstairs is up to something. There's a glint in her eye.

Valentine You can't just leave corpses lying around in the hallway.

Natalia He's still fresh.

Valentine So? Hang on ... no, I am not feeding on that.

Natalia Oh come on, I saved him especially. I thought you might be hungry, are you?

Valentine What?

Natalia Hungry?

Valentine No ... Why would I be hungry? I have just returned from feeding, therefore quenching my hunger ... so ... no I'm not hungry, why on earth would I be hungry? ... mmm? Why do you ask?

Natalia Because I know you.

Pause

Hungry?

Long pause

Valentine Starving.

Natalia Thought so. (*She gives him the bottle of blood*)

Valentine I was so close, Natalia. I found the jugular and everything. Then she woke up.

Valentine drinks

Natalia That's not a problem. How many times have I told you, once you've sunk your fangs into the neck it's only a matter of seconds before they go all woozy and limp.

Valentine I didn't exactly get the chance.

Natalia What do you mean?

Valentine They were all poised, and then I felt a bit faint.

Natalia Faint?

Valentine Yes ... but I did break the skin ... eventually. She bled and everything.

Natalia And what did you do?

Pause

Natalia Valentine?
Valentine Offer to clean her up.
Natalia Valentine!
Valentine What? I panicked. I'm not as composed as you are. I see blood and I go all squiggly.
Natalia You have no problems with a bottle.
Valentine Well there's no ... ooozing or flesh involved with bottled blood.
Natalia Babies drink from bottles. Counts don't!
Valentine Oh, here we go. I know I'm Count Valentino from Castle Vallos in some obscure little Eastern European village whose name I can't pronounce.
Natalia You can't deny your heritage.
Valentine No I can't ... I can't even pronounce the name of the village I grew up in. My God! I don't have any heritage!
Natalia Don't be silly, you are Count Valentino, you have Castle Vallos, you are a member of one of the most fearsome vampire families in the world, you feed on the living and you are immortal!
Valentine No, listen. I am Valentine, not Valentino, not Count just Valentine, I have no castle ... I have a flat ... in Putney, I am not fearsome ... I am a florist and I don't feed on the living, I feed from bottles you bring me from your feeding sessions and I may be immortal ... but ... I ... err ... yeah.
Natalia What?
Valentine What?
Natalia You trailed off after immortal.
Valentine I did ... but did you have to point it out? Can you pronounce the name of the village I come from?
Natalia It's not important!
Valentine Ha, ha! You see, nobody knows it. Even the people that live there probably don't know its name!
Natalia You're straying from the point.
Valentine Which is?
Natalia You are a vampire ...
Valentine Ah, vampire-human hybrid thank you very much. I'm special.

Pause. They look at each other

What? I am. A vampire-human hybrid going on to be a full vampire, that's special ——

Natalia Silence! You are a vampire.

Valentine I ——

Natalia Hush. You are vampire and as a vampire you must feed. You must get over this phobia of yours and feed properly! (*She sits down*)

Valentine I'm trying. I've got my priorities right. I sharpen my fangs every night.

Natalia It's no longer just a teething problem. You have to feed properly soon. You're my baby brother and I like to look after you but I can't keep saving you. I'm going to have to be cruel to be kind.

Valentine I know ... I am trying.

Natalia Oh I know, don't get upset ... come here. (*She stands and hugs him*) You go get some sleep. (*She kisses his forehead*)

Valentine starts to leave

Natalia What you doing for breakfast?

Valentine Oh ... I ... err.

Natalia There's a bottle in the fridge.

Valentine Thank you.

Valentine leaves

Lights fade

SCENE 2

Valentine's flat, the bathroom. Night

Valentine, in his pyjamas, is standing C, *facing front. He behaves as though he is looking into a mirror*

Valentine (*closing his eyes*) OK ... deep breaths. Fearsome vampire, I'm a terrifying, blood-drinking monster ... fearsome vampire. (*He opens his eyes, strikes a pose and continues to strike poses*) This would be so much easier if I had a reflection. Guess I could internalize. (*He closes his eyes*) OK fangs, there they are, hi guys, scary arms, oh yeah, hypno eyes ... oooh, twirly.

Valentine becomes hypnotized. His eyes open. He stands open-mouthed

Natalia (*off*) Valentine? Are you in there? Valentine? Valentine? What are you up to? Answer me? Valentine?

Pause

(*Off*) I hope you're decent.

Natalia enters in her pyjamas

Oh not again! How many times, never think about your hypno eyes while internalizing. Oh Valentine, I love you dearly but you really do continue to make schoolboy errors. Right come over here.

She pulls him away from the mirror and sits him down on the floor

Valentine! Valentine! Look at me!

She starts tapping his face. His head falls limp. She holds his head to her own

Look into my eyes! Come on. Look!
Valentine (*laughing*) You're silly. Where's my spatula? Oooh, tiles! Nice tiles, good tiles. (*Laughing*) Silly lady ... pretty, pretty tiles ...

Valentine falls forward. Natalia catches his head and rests it down

Natalia leaves

Valentine mumbles incoherently

Natalia enters with a bottle of blood

She puts some on her fingers and puts it on Valentine's lips. He wakes

Oh hello. How are you?

Natalia just looks at him. Valentine looks around

I did it again didn't I?
Natalia You did. How many times have I told you? Thinking about your hypno eyes while internalizing is never a good idea!
Valentine (*standing*) How am I supposed to know whether they work or not?
Natalia You just know, if a victim goes all wiggly when you stare at them, they work, job done!
Valentine But I need to practise and my eyes are a key part of the whole fearsome vampire image.

Natalia Well, now you know yours work. No need to practise them anymore.

Pause

Valentine Did I go wiggly?
Natalia You did.
Valentine Did I mention the spatula?
Natalia You did.
Valentine Tiles?
Natalia Oh yes.
Valentine I see.
Natalia You do, but when you internalize try not to think about your eyes anymore, OK?
Valentine OK. What's the time?
Natalia Ten-thirty.
Valentine Work! I've got to go!
Natalia Aren't you forgetting something?
Valentine Oh. (*He kisses her on the cheek and begins to leave*)
Natalia ...What was that?
Valentine A kiss.
Natalia Why?
Valentine Well, that's what people do.
Natalia You never do.
Valentine Don't I?
Natalia No. We're brother and sister not ... husband and wife.
Valentine I'm awfully sorry.
Natalia Don't worry about it. You're still forgetting something very important.
Valentine What?

Natalia looks at him and gestures towards his pyjamas

Natalia New uniform?
Valentine Ah yes, better get changed.

Valentine exits

Natalia Be back before sunrise, remember nobody likes a crispy Count. See you later, hypno boy.

Lights fade

SCENE 3

Hayley's flat. Evening

Hayley is sitting in a chair in pyjamas. She is on the phone

Hayley Someone else? You're seeing someone else? Well so am I.
(*Pause*) No, you don't know him. (*Pause*) Why? ... Because there is
nobody else, I was just trying to retaliate. How dare you? The fact
you break up with me via text, that really tells me what kind of man
you are! Bet you didn't expect me to call, did you? (*Pause*) Don't you
say that! Don't you dare do the "I'm glad you did" bit ... I'm glad
we're over, because you are balding, have a pot belly, wear Y-fronts,
snore like a really big thing and ... well ... yeah. What was that? Hang
on is she there? Is she there? Put her on the phone ... put her on ...
(*louder*) put her on the phone! Well I'll shout then, hey bitch! You fat
boyfriend-stealing slut, I hope your children are fat and ugly. I don't
believe you, what's going on? Why aren't you saying anything? Why
are you breathing so heavily ... Oh, my, God! You fat bastard! (*She
slams the phone down*)

She storms out of her flat

Black-out

SCENE 4

The florist shop. Night

Valentine is under the counter. Hayley enters

Hayley Hello? Anybody here? Hello?

Valentine pops up from behind the counter

Valentine Oh ... hello, yes, hello ... err ... hello.
Hayley You're open?
Valentine Yes.
Hayley But you're never open ... during the day?
Valentine The day, no. You see, I'm allergic.
Hayley What, to sunlight?
Valentine Ye —— no, just err clouds.
Hayley Clouds?

Valentine Yes ... white ... fluffy ... clouds.

Hayley OK ... each to his own. Since you're open I'll buy something. I know nothing at all about flowers, but I'm looking for something ...

Valentine Really, what?

Hayley Flowers ... you are a florist after all, right?

Valentine Of course. Flowers, right. Flowers for an occasion? Birthday? New Job? Engagement? Wedding? First Child? Anniversary? (*Pause*) Funeral?

Hayley No I've just moved into a flat and I want to spruce it up a bit, and thought some flowers would be nice ... Alive, preferably.

Valentine Mmm. Indeed they would be. What are your favourite colours?

Hayley Well ... mainly darker colours, reds, purples that sort of thing.

Valentine Right, let's see what we have. (*He dives under the counter and starts looking for flowers*)

Hayley Do you own this place?

Valentine (*popping up*) I do. (*He dives back underneath the counter*)

Hayley Isn't it expensive?

Valentine (*popping up*) What? (*He dives back underneath the counter*)

Hayley To run I mean? You must make a bit of money, but since you're closed during the day due to a cloud-related illness (*she shakes her head*) how do you make enough money?

Valentine (*popping up*) Well I have a bit of money put away. (*He dives back underneath the counter*)

Hayley Really, I thought you would have made your money on orders, you're not exactly overstocked.

Valentine stops, realizing what he's just said, stands and turns to Hayley

Valentine Well we do ... yes we make money on orders.

Hayley No, it's too late now. You said you have money put away.

Valentine ... Yes ... well I inherited some money, some of which is invested in the shop.

Hayley Some of which? Rich family then?

Valentine No, not really ... I'm just a regular guy who runs a ... florist.

Hayley Regular guys don't run florists.

Valentine They don't?

Hayley Not usually no. When I came in I thought it was a little unusual to see a male florist. That and the fact that you are open in the middle of the night.

Valentine Unusual in a creepy way or a refreshing way?

Hayley Refreshing way. I don't find you at all creepy, should I?

Valentine Well ...

Hayley Anyway you don't seem to have quite what I want in stock.

Valentine Oh, I'm sorry.

Hayley No need to apologise.

Valentine I'm sure I can acquire more stock. If I did, what would you like?

Hayley Whatever you choose, I trust your judgment. Even if you are a creepy male florist.

Valentine I thought you said you didn't find me creepy.

Hayley I don't. I was joking, do you take everything so literally?

Valentine Usually ... yes.

Hayley OK.

Valentine goes behind the counter and brings out a notebook and a pen. He hands it to Hayley

Valentine If you could just give me your name and a contact phone number?

She takes the book and pen

Hayley Sure. (*She writes down her details*)

Valentine waits, awkwardly. Hayley hands back the book

Since I gave you mine could I have yours?

Valentine looks confused

It's Hayley. Pleased to meet you ...

Valentine Oh ... err ... Valentine.

They shake hands

Hayley Nice name.

Valentine Thank you ... I'll be in touch when your flowers are ready. Will you be able to collect?

Hayley Usual opening hours?

Valentine Yes.

Hayley Well, I just hope the flowers are worth it. Bye.

Lights fade as Hayley leaves

SCENE 5

Valentine's flat, the living-room. Early evening

Natalia and Valentine are sitting on a sofa. Natalia is knitting. Valentine is staring into space. There is a long pause

Valentine Natalia?
Natalia (*not looking up*) Mmm?
Valentine Do you ever get ... well ...
Natalia (*not looking up*) What?
Valentine Lonely?

Long pause

Natalia (*putting down her knitting*) Where did that come from?
Valentine I've just been getting a little bored lately. I go to work, I come home, I go to feed, I go all squiggly when I see blood, I fail, I come home, I drink from a bottle, I go to bed, I get up, I practise being a proper vampire, I hypnotize myself, I go to work, I come home, I go to feed, I go all squiggly ...
Natalia OK, OK. I get it.
Valentine It's all so repetitive ... and it makes me feel very alone and empty.
Natalia What about me, don't I keep you company?
Valentine Yes, but you're ... you know ... you. (*He looks at Natalia*) Don't get me wrong. I love your company but I never meet anyone else ... well, not usually when they're awake anyway, I crave a bit of variety. I want to meet more people.
Natalia What about the flower shop? You meet people in there ... don't you?
Valentine Well, with vampiric opening hours, I'm never exactly inundated with customers, but tonight I had a customer!
Natalia You did? Who's my clever little vampire florist?
Valentine Stop it!
Natalia Sorry, can't resist it. Who knows, she may spread the word and you'll become a world renowned florist?
Valentine Hardly, the flower business isn't exactly ——
Natalia Blooming?
Valentine Well done. As I was saying ... one customer in God knows how many ... years.
Natalia So business is slow, the lesson here? Don't try.

Valentine Look, business being slow isn't really a problem, but the lack of customer interaction does make my existence a little empty and if I'm going to have an immortal existence, I have to spice it up a little.

Natalia Once your vampiric powers fully kick in, things will change.

Valentine Will they? What if they don't? What if I've become too civilized? What if I'm the first ... (*Pause*) ... domesticated vampire ... like a cat?

Natalia Don't be silly. Once you're behaving like a true vampire, you'll close the florist and we'll strike fear into the hearts of hundreds. People will tremble at the mere mention of our names. We will be legends. Every generation will know our names and our reign of terror will make us the most formidable vampires in history!

Long pause

Well, say something?

Valentine Cool.

Black-out

SCENE 6

The florist shop. Night

Hayley enters

Hayley Hello, anyone here? I'm here to pick up an order, I was here a couple of days ago? I got a message on my phone, sorry I didn't pick up I was, well ... asleep.

There is a sneeze off stage

Hello, is there someone back there?

Valentine emerges. His eyes are streaming and he is holding a pack of tissues

You look terrible, have you got a cold?

Valentine No. (*He sneezes*) It's hay fever.

Hayley Hay fever?

Valentine Yes.

Hayley But you're a florist.

Valentine True.
Hayley A florist with hay fever, that's a little ironic don't you think?
Valentine Well, maybe, but it's only certain flowers.
Hayley What kind of flowers?
Valentine These. (*He sneezes*)

He holds up a bouquet and hands it to Hayley

Hayley Oh they're perfect! How much do I owe you?
Valentine On the house.
Hayley Oh thank you. You sure that's OK?
Valentine Abso... (*he sneezes*) ... lutely.
Hayley That's very sweet, thank you.

Hayley goes to leave

Valentine Erm.

Hayley turns back

Hayley What?
Valentine Would you like to maybe erm ... see each other again ... possibly eat ... food and drink ... drink? You don't have to ... I mean you can say no but ——
Hayley Are you asking me out ... on a date?
Valentine No ... I might be ... would you like me to?
Hayley Sure, sounds like fun. When do you want to meet?
Valentine Sunset?
Hayley So say seven?
Valentine Sounds good.
Hayley Where do you want to go? There's a nice Italian down the round?
Valentine Perfect.
Hayley Cool, well seven at the Italian, see you then.

She leaves

Valentine stands alone. He sneezes

Black-out

Scene 7

Valentine's flat, the living-room. Evening

Valentine is lying at one end of the sofa watching television. Natalia enters

Natalia What you watching?
Valentine TV.
Natalia I can see that, what's on?
Valentine Movie.
Natalia What kind of movie?
Valentine Vampire movie.
Natalia What's it called?
Valentine Blood of something. Innocence, lust something like that.
Natalia Well which is it, innocence or lust?
Valentine Neither, it's something like that.
Natalia You really are a fountain of knowledge.
Valentine Thank you.

Natalia sits next to him, he snuggles up to her, as a child would to its mother. Pause

Valentine Natalia?
Natalia (*cautiously*) Yes?
Valentine Why say it like that?
Natalia Like what?
Valentine Like that, with a sense of impending doom?
Natalia No reason, but whenever you use my name it indicates the start of a deep conversation.

Long pause

Valentine Natalia?
Natalia Yes Valentine?
Valentine ... nothing.

Pause

Natalia Did you sell those flowers today?
Valentine Have you ever been out with a mortal?
Natalia Selling flowers to relationships with mortals, bit of a topic jump there, but ... yes I've been out with many mortals ... men, mostly.

Valentine Anyone you didn't feast upon?

Natalia Erm, no, fed from them all. Why?

Valentine The lady that picked up the flowers, I'm taking her to dinner tomorrow night.

Natalia And she's on the menu ... mmm?

Valentine What? No! I couldn't eat anyone I know.

Natalia That shouldn't make a difference. Where you going?

Valentine She suggested the Italian place just down from the shop, near the shopping centre, which is near the post office, next door to the supermarket which is ——

Natalia OK, OK. Hang on? Did you say the Italian place?

Valentine Yes.

Natalia Italian.

Valentine Yes.

Natalia As in garlic?

Valentine Ye —— Oh.

Natalia Precisely. Why didn't you say no?

Valentine I forgot. I can't be expected to remember everything.

Natalia What are you going to do?

Valentine Well, I should be OK if I don't eat any garlic and try not to smell it directly.

Natalia Trying to avoid garlic in an Italian restaurant. That's not going to be easy. It's like trying to avoid getting wet when out in the rain ... impossible!

Valentine Not if you have an umbrella.

Natalia Valentine!

Valentine Look, if I say I'm allergic to garlic then they'll have to accommodate me.

Natalia Yeah, tell them any direct contact with garlic causes you to err ... die.

Valentine Die! I didn't think it was that serious.

Natalia Well, that's only if you eat it, but direct contact or smelling it will make you very sick.

Valentine I will have to take my chances.

Natalia Just go somewhere else ... then take her home and feed.

Valentine No! This is the first person I've had proper interaction with in a long time and I don't want to mess it up. Who knows, this may stop me from feeling so alone.

Natalia Valentine, she's mortal.

Valentine So?

Natalia You're a vampire. There's a slight compatibility problem there don't you think?

Valentine Well there doesn't have to be.

Natalia Watch the movie.

They both look at the television

Natalia Who is distressed in this scenario?

Valentine The girl.

Natalia True. Now what is the vampire doing?

Valentine Kind of growling and snarling and ugh! Drooling.

Natalia Exactly. Now the reason he is doing this is because he is attracted to the lady in question. A vampire's lust is a dangerous thing. Once you get intimate, bang — you go all snarly and the drool cascades from your mouth like a waterfall.

Valentine Is that true?

Natalia Could be ... Look, even considering any sort of romantic involvement with a mortal is a bad move.

Valentine It's dinner. Food ... drink, conversation.

Natalia At night.

Valentine So?

Natalia Valentine, if I didn't know better I'd question you being a vampire at all. You know the importance of night, the power of the moon, what happens to us, our bloodlust?

Valentine Whoah! Slow down there, your bloodlust, not mine. Sure I like the moon and may get a little excited by it, but I don't start craving blood.

Natalia Not yet, but you will.

Valentine Maybe ... but I don't at the moment and I'm not going to be eternally lonely just because of what might happen.

Natalia Well what you going to eat?

Valentine Well. A garlic-free Bolognese perhaps. It doesn't really matter since my taste buds aren't as sensitive when eating "mortal" food.

Natalia Just a hint of garlic and you'll be vomiting and breaking out in rashes in all sorts of colours.

Valentine Therefore I just have to make sure that no garlic goes anywhere near my plate. I have to appear perfectly normal.

Natalia Normal?

Valentine Yep, perfectly normal. Now if you excuse me I am going to prepare for my c ... c ... prepare for sleep.

He leaves

Natalia goes to the phone

Natalia (*on the phone*) Hello, sorry to call you so close to sunrise but we may have a problem.

Black-out

SCENE 8

The restaurant. Night

Valentine and Hayley are sitting at a table opposite one another. There is a candle in between them. They are looking at menus. They close them and put them down then look at each other. Hayley moves the candle

Hayley Shall we get some garlic bread?
Valentine Oh ... I ... erm ... well ...
Hayley What?
Valentine I'm allergic to garlic.
Hayley Really?
Valentine Yes.
Hayley Well isn't that going to be a problem, what with this being an Italian restaurant? Why didn't you say anything?
Valentine I forgot.
Hayley You forgot?
Valentine Yes.
Hayley That you have an allergic reaction to garlic?
Valentine I was sneezing so much I didn't remember.
Hayley That reminds me, thank you again for the rose. It's been a very long time since I've been given a rose, especially one that was bought before the date, not during it. Never really understood how that works? Buying a rose at the end of or during a date? From a seller with a soggy dripping bucket? Seems a bit cheap to me really, so thank you.

Pause

I guess we can skip the garlic bread. What you going to eat?
Valentine Vegetarian cannelloni without the garlic.
Hayley I'll have the ravioli ... oh without the garlic of course. Shall we get some wine?
Valentine I don't drink ... wine.
Hayley Oh.

Long pause

Valentine Well, not red, but white should be fine.

Black-out

Valentine's flat, the living-room. Night

We hear a plane landing and the flapping of wings. Lights come up on the living-room in Valentine's flat. Natalia, Marianne and Vincent enter. Marianne is pulling a suitcase. On top of it is a large black hold-all. Vincent's clothes are soaked through

Vincent Why, whenever I fly to London, it always rains? Where is Valentine?

Marianne Well, if you must travel as a bat, rain can be a bother.

Pause

Vincent Where is my son?

Natalia He's at dinner ... with her.

Vincent What! Why didn't you stop him?

Natalia I tried.

Marianne I don't know what all the fuss is about, it is only a date.

Vincent Where are they?

Natalia At the Italian restaurant down the road.

Marianne Italian?

Vincent Oh my God!

Natalia I know, I warned him, but he wouldn't listen to me. What are you going to do?

Vincent I have no choice. I must go to the restaurant.

Vincent goes over to the hold-all and opens it

Natalia What about the garl ——

Before she can finish he pulls out a gas mask

Oh.

Pause

Erm, do you always travel with a gas mask?

Marianne When dealing with Valentine he likes to be prepared for any eventuality.

Vincent I go.

Marianne Yes, dear.

Vincent leaves

Black-out

SCENE 10

The restaurant

Time has passed. Two half filled wine glasses are on the table with plates. Valentine and Hayley have finished their meals. Hayley fills the glasses

Hayley So you're European then?

Valentine Technically yes, but I came here when I was eleven or twelve and almost completely lost my accent. That's enough about me though. Where are you from?

Hayley Well I'm English and grew up in Middlesex. I went to university in America and did consider living there, but after a few weeks back here I realized I couldn't leave. I just love the diversity in London, so many interesting people, creepy male florists for example, that turn out to be fascinating, charming, rich Europeans who suffer from hay fever and can't eat garlic.

Valentine And it's not everyday I meet charming people like you. Don't really meet anyone in that shop, not much call for a florist in this area.

Hayley Well, opening in the dead of night is probably not helping sales. You could open in the day?

Valentine But ... clouds.

Hayley You seriously don't expect me to believe you are allergic to clouds.

Valentine But I am ...

Hayley Come on ... look, if ——

Suddenly Vincent, in a gas mask, arrives and places garlic bread on the table

I'm sorry we didn't order any bread, we requested the bill.

Vincent leaves

Valentine starts convulsing

Valentine, are you —— ? Oh God! Valentine!

Valentine is struggling not to vomit. Vincent returns with a plate of mushrooms

Why are you bringing all this? We didn't order any of it and look at him, he's allergic to garlic ... and why are you wearing a gas mask?

Valentine, still convulsing more violently and struggling to breathe, moves over to Vincent

Before he gets a chance to get too close Vincent leaves

Valentine falls to the floor

Hayley Valentine? Valentine?
Valentine I need to get some air.
Hayley Of course.

Hayley leaves some cash on the table and helps Valentine to his feet

They exit

Lights fade

Scene 11

The street. Night

Valentine and Hayley enter wearing coats

Hayley Well, this is me. Thanks for walking me home.
Valentine My pleasure.
Hayley You're quite the gentleman. I still can't believe they brought us garlic after all we said to the waiter.
Valentine I'm sorry about that.
Hayley You have nothing to apologize for. It was the waiter's fault, not yours. What was he thinking? Also, why was he wearing a gas mask?
Valentine I have no idea.
Hayley That was quite a reaction. I thought you were going to die. I have never seen such an adverse reaction to just the smell of something. I dread to think what might have happened if you accidentally ate some.
Valentine Yes, well, like I said, I'm sorry.
Hayley And like I said, it wasn't your fault. Would you like to come up for coffee?

Pause

Oh, was that really as clichéd as it sounds? Well, clichéd or not it's a
genuine offer. Would you like to come up for a beverage? Nope ... still
sounds cheesy.
Valentine I should probably be getting home.
Hayley Oh.
Valentine Well, good-night.

*After a few moments they hug. Then they look at each other for a moment
and kiss*

Hayley We will see each other again, right?
Valentine Absolutely.

They kiss again

Hayley Hey, Valentine?
Valentine What?
Hayley Don't look now, but there's a cloud.

Black-out

SCENE 12

Valentine's flat, the living-room. Night

Valentine enters

Valentine Talking to the folks again?
Natalia How'd you guess?
Valentine Your face says it all. What do they want?
Natalia Oh just the usual.
Valentine I see. Did you tell them about my date?
Natalia Well ... I had to ...
Valentine Natalia! Why? You know as well as I do that they're never
    gonna let this go!
Natalia I had to tell them, this is a big deal.

   Vincent enters

Vincent A very big deal.
Valentine Dad? When? What?

Vincent Good to see you too, son.
Valentine But, you, here, wha ... I don ——
Vincent As coherent as ever, I see.
Valentine When did you arrive?
Vincent I've been here a good few hours.
Valentine A few hours! Hang on, were you —— ?

Vincent reveals the gas mask he has been holding behind his back

What on earth did you think you were doing?
Vincent Only what was needed.
Valentine Needed? You almost killed me.

Marianne enters

Marianne What?
Valentine Mum! Oh perfect, this is absolutely perfect! Is there anyone else hiding behind there? Anyone?
Marianne Valentine, what did your father do?
Valentine He gave me garlic.
Vincent I put it on their table.
Valentine Yeah, but still. Hayley and I were having an enjoyable garlic-free evening, then you bundle in and almost ruin everything.
Natalia Almost?
Vincent You mean she didn't panic and run away.
Valentine No. In fact we're seeing each other again.
Natalia No!
Vincent You can't!
Marianne That's lovely.

Pause as everyone looks at Marianne

Valentine Mother, Father ... Natalia, if you'll excuse me, I'm going for a walk. As I trust you will be staying in a nearby hotel I shall bid you goodnight.
Marianne But Valentine, we have only just got here.
Valentine Exactly, and within a few hours an attempt has already been made on my life.
Vincent Don't be so dramatic.
Valentine Good-night Mother, Father ... Natalia.
Marianne Where are you going?
Valentine Long walk on to a short pointy stick.
Marianne A stake?
Valentine (*confused*) No thank you, I'm not hungry.

Valentine exits

Marianne Valentine?
Natalia It's all right, he'll be back later, I'll talk to him. You better go find a hotel for the morning. Of course you are welcome to stay ——
Vincent We go.
Marianne Yes, dear.

Black-out

SCENE 13

Valentine's flat, the living-room. Very early morning: it is dark

Valentine enters trying to be very quiet. Suddenly the light comes on. Natlaia is standing by the switch. Valentine jumps

Natalia Did you kiss?
Valentine Natalia!
Natalia Don't be bashful, did you kiss?
Valentine Yes and it was very nice, better than I expected in fact.
Natalia Don't get big-headed. It's a natural skill that all vampires inherit at a very young age, it's due to the over-developed mouths we have what with our fangs and over-developed tongue.
Valentine Yeah but my fangs weren't extended or anything.
Natalia Course they weren't, you weren't planning to bite but the development of our mouths still improve our kissing abilities.
Valentine My first fully-fledged vampire skill.
Natalia Minor skill, you would have developed this by the age of three.
Valentine You always have to shoot my achievements down in flames.
Natalia It's not an achievement, it's a given. (*Long pause*) Are you going to see her again?
Valentine Definitely.
Natalia I see.
Valentine Yes you do and you call our parents. How could you? You know what Dad's like.
Natalia He cares and knows as well I do that vampires and mortals don't mix.
Valentine My mother was mortal when they met, when I was conceived in fact, hence my half-and-half situation.
Natalia Exactly, you weren't planned, you are a vampire anomaly, everyone was surprised you were even born.

Valentine I well ... thank you for that. It's a good job I'm immortal because I may well have killed myself by now. But being half human I can forgive you and appreciate this is quite a big step for me and you are slightly nervous, perhaps a tiny bit jealous that I have someone else to talk to.
Natalia I am not jealous.
Valentine Yes well whatever it is will have to wait, I'm off to nap in my ... c ... my cof ... my ...
Natalia Say it!
Valentine Don't want to. It's creepy.
Natalia It's where you sleep.

Pause

Valentine Coffin, I sleep in a coffin, you happy now?

Valentine exits

Long pause

Valentine enters

Natalia! Oh God it's horrible!
Natalia What?
Valentine There's a roach in my coffin!

Long pause

Hold me.

Natalia goes over to him. Black-out

(*In the darkness*) Can I sleep in your coffin today?

SCENE 14

Valentine's flat, the living-room. Early evening

Valentine and Natalia are sitting on the sofa. Valentine is in his pyjamas. They are watching television

Valentine Does that happen?
Natalia Does what happen?

Valentine When a friendly vampire makes love with a mortal do they go all growly and snarly ... oh and start attacking everyone?
Natalia I'm not sure.
Valentine Has it happened to you?
Natalia Am I all snarly and growly?
Valentine Well ... no.
Natalia There you go then.
Valentine That's a relief.

Long pause

Natalia Then of course I'm a female.
Valentine What?
Natalia I'm not a male vampire. That's an entirely different ball game.
Valentine Is it?
Natalia Absolutely. Each vampire is different, you're living proof of that. Maybe that's your turning point. Once you make love, then wham! You'll be a fully fledged vampire!
Valentine No that can't be true, it's just this movie.
Natalia It happens in a lot of movies, also mostly after love making, the victim either dies or becomes a vampire, you've noticed that, haven't you?
Valentine Well yeah, but ——
Natalia There's no buts. Making love changes a vampire. So be careful.
Valentine What?
Natalia Well when you're with your friend.
Valentine Hayley.
Natalia Whatever.
Valentine Her name is Hayley.
Natalia Sure Hayley. Make sure ... you know.
Valentine What? You're making me extremely nervous.
Natalia No need to be nervous, just don't get into any tricky situations ... like ... Oh , I don't know, a kiss, for example.
Valentine Oh here we go, was wondering when we'd get round to that? What's wrong with a kiss?
Natalia It often leads to other things. Anyway there are other problems with the scenario, for example,   you're a vampire, Nosferatu, you drink blood. Fair enough from bottles, but soon Harry ——
Valentine Hayley.
Natalia Will be nothing more than your next meal!

Valentine says nothing. He starts to tremble

Natalia What's with the trembling?
Valentine Sorry Natalia but I'm fairly alarmed here, right now.
Natalia Well you don't have to be, you know what you have to do.
Valentine Do I?
Natalia Break it off ... now!
Valentine It's two-thirty in the morning.
Natalia Well, tomorrow then.
Valentine No, can't tomorrow.
Natalia Why not?
Valentine Meeting her tomorrow.
Natalia That's the perfect opportunity!
Valentine I don't want to break it off.
Natalia Well, if you wanna run the risk?
Valentine Exactly, it's a risk, might not happen.
Natalia Know what I'd be putting my money on.
Valentine I like her and I like being around her, I don't care what's involved!
Natalia I'll remind you of that when you're nibbling on her forearm.
Valentine Natalia!
Natalia What? It's gonna happen.
Valentine No it won't, I like having someone else to care for. Something to look after, to protect.
Natalia Do you remember that hamster I bought you for you to ... look after, to protect?
Valentine Oh yeah. Sookie.
Natalia Do you remember what happened to Sookie?
Valentine ... erm.
Natalia You ate her.
Valentine I was having a rough time and I was hungry.
Natalia And you won't feel hungry when with Harry?
Valentine I don't need to stand here all day and listen to you talk about my eating habits. I loved Sookie.
Natalia I still hear her squeaking now. As you ——
Valentine I'm going for a walk and then I'm going to see Harry ... Hayley.
Natalia In your pajamas?
Valentine Yes ... well, no obviously, I'll change first ... oh goodbye, Natalia.
Natalia Hang on, what should I tell the folks if they drop by?
Valentine What does it matter? You'll tell them everything anyway. I mean, I meet someone other than you and they're on the first plane here ... well, except Dad doing his bat thing. Goodbye, Natalia.
Natalia Bye ... remember, no clinching!

Black-out

SCENE 15

Hayley's flat

Valentine and Hayley are together. Hayley is lying in Valentine's arms

Hayley I mean how polite are you? Asking to be invited in?
Valentine Hayley?
Hayley Yes?
Valentine Are we clinching?
Hayley Not really.
Valentine Oh.

Long pause

  Are you sure?
Hayley (*sitting up*) What's the matter?
Valentine Nothing.
Hayley What's up?
Valentine It's nothing.
Hayley So there is something then?
Valentine I'm just a little unsure. (*He stands*)
Hayley About what?
Valentine This.
Hayley What do you mean this?
Valentine Well ... this us.
Hayley (*standing*) Us? You're not breaking up with me are you?
Valentine No, of course not.
Hayley (*sitting back down*) Oh. What is it then?
Valentine I'm just scared.
Hayley Of what?

Valentine says nothing

  Look, I like you, I enjoy being around you. You like me, and today
it's been nice just being together hasn't it? Even if we were almost
clinching?
Valentine I'm just worrying ——
Hayley Don't. You don't have to.

Pause. She moves towards Valentine. They hug — it is awkward

Hayley What?

Valentine I need to tell you something.

Hayley OK.

Valentine Before we get too involved. (*He stands and turns his back to her*)

Hayley What is it?

Valentine (*turning back to her*) I'm not like other guys.

Hayley I know, that's why I like you.

Valentine I mean I'm different.

Hayley (*standing*) What are you talking about? (*Pause*) Oh hang on. You're not trying to tell me that every full moon you turn into The Wolfman are you?

Valentine Well ... not him, no.

Hayley Oh come here.

They hug, then they kiss

Now what was it you wanted to tell me?

Valentine It ... it's not important.

Hayley You feeling a bit more positive about us now?

Valentine Yes.

Hayley Well you've seen mine, when am I going to see yours?

Valentine What?

Hayley (*giggling*) Your place. When am I going to see your place?

Valentine My place?

Hayley Your habitat, abode, nest, dwelling place, where you live?

Valentine Oh that kind of place. Tomorrow night for ... dinner?

Hayley Tomorrow night?

Valentine Yes. As in the night after the night tonight? So not tonight's night but tomorrow night's night. So tomorrow night not tonight night but tomorrow ——

Hayley OK stop. You're confusing yourself ... and me. So tomorrow night, yes?

Valentine Yes.

Hayley Just us?

Valentine My sister may be there.

Hayley OK, that's cool. If she's anything like you, it's going to be a great night.

Valentine (*to himself*) ... and my parents.

Hayley What?

Valentine Nothing.

Black-out

SCENE 16

Valentine's flat, the living-room

Valentine and Natalia are sitting on the sofa. Valentine is wearing a dressing gown as a smoking jacket and is holding a pipe

Natalia Aren't you feeling a little overdressed?
Valentine What do you mean?
Natalia The smoking jacket, the pipe?
Valentine (*standing*) Well, it's what I always wear.
Natalia No it's not.
Valentine Nothing wrong with a change of image.

Long pause

Natalia When's she arriving?
Valentine How'd you guess?
Natalia You've been cooking all day and now the new image.
Valentine Yes well, Hayley ... not she ... Hayley is arriving soon. I thought you might be going out to feed.
Natalia You thought I might or hoped I would?
Valentine Well it was a bit of both.
Natalia Well I'm not going anywhere ... now.
Valentine OK, but please try not to ruin this for me.
Natalia I will only be myself.
Valentine (*sitting*) That's what I'm worried about. Please try and be pleasant ... Please?
Natalia You know how I feel about this relationship, Valentine and ... and ... Oh look, I can't be stern with you when you're wearing that ridiculous dressing gown.
Valentine It's a smoking jacket.
Natalia It's ... a dressing gown. Take it off.
Valentine No.

There is a knock at the door

   Natalia exits

Valentine Please no.

   Natalia enters with Vincent and Marianne

Vincent Good-evening.

Marianne Hello Valentine. Erm is that a dressing gown? And a pipe?

Valentine It is a pipe and you smoke a pipe hence the smoking jacket.

Natalia Yes, Mum, it's a dressing gown.

Vincent Take off the dressing gown and put away the pipe, you look ridiculous.

Valentine But ——

Vincent Now!

Valentine Yes, Father!

Vincent When is she arriving?

Valentine How do you know?

Vincent gestures towards Natalia

Of course. Why can't you just let me have a normal, healthy relationship?

Natalia With a mortal?

Valentine Yes a mortal, what's the problem?

Natalia There are all sorts of problems, you are too different. Look, you know how your father and I feel about this relationship and I'm not going to hide my concerns. I can't, I have your interests at heart.

Valentine But surely you want me to be happy?

Natalia (*standing*) I do, but I know this will end up making you unhappy.

Valentine How can you possibly know that?

Vincent Think about it. You are a vampire, she isn't, you need blood, she needs it too but she doesn't have to consume it, you do.

Natalia It's not the most appealing concept, not if you're mortal anyway.

Valentine As long as she doesn't see me consuming it.

Natalia She will at some point.

Valentine Not tonight though.

Natalia Well ... don't be so sure.

Valentine Please don't do this, Natalia!

Natalia If you can't nip this in the bud, maybe I'll have to help.

Valentine I don't want your help. I don't want this nipped in the bud. I like her, I really like her. Mum, surely you understand?

Marianne Of course I do, but your father and ... sister make valid points.

Valentine But you were mortal when you met Dad?

Marianne That was a very long time ago, Valentine, and the world was a very different place.

Natalia It can't work, it won't. I'm going to have to end this for your own good.

Valentine My own good? How can this be good for me?

Natalia I'm not going to keep telling you the same thing, you know why it's a problem.
Valentine I'm going to the bathroom ... wash my nails.
Marianne Your nails.
Valentine ... Yes.
Natalia No hypnotizing yourself.
Valentine (*sarcastically*) Oh ha, ha, ha ... (*sheepishly*) OK.

He exits

Lights fade on one half of the stage

Vincent So when will we meet this girl?
Natalia Soon, judging by Valentine's nervousness.
Marianne What's her name?
Natalia Harry.
Valentine (*off*) Hayley!
Marianne Maybe we should leave, dear. I'm sure Natalia has this in hand, we don't want to intimidate the poor girl.
Natalia I can handle it.
Vincent No, I must see her.
Marianne OK, but after she has arrived we leave.

Long pause. Transformation sound

Valentine (*off*) Oh no, please no.

The doorbell rings

(*Off*) Oh perfect, this is just perfect.
Natalia What's the problem?
Valentine (*off*) I'm gonna be in here for a while.
Marianne What, why?

The doorbell rings again

Valentine enters the bathroom area

Marianne enters the bathroom area and the bathroom lights come up. Valentine has almost turned into a bat. He has one wing and ears

Marianne Oh, Valentine.
Valentine I was about to wash my nails, then suddenly ... It's just nerves. It'll wear off soon.

Natalia (*entering the bathroom*) What on earth?
Valentine I'll be fine soon.
Natalia Well she's here. Should I send her away?
Marianne I think maybe ——
Valentine No! Just stall her for a few minutes, could you?
Natalia Oh ... I'm sure we'll be able to find something to talk about ...
Valentine Don't you dare! Mum, tell her!
Natalia You just concentrate on regaining human form.

The doorbell rings

Valentine Get the door.

Natalia and Marianne exit the bathroom

  Natalia exits

Vincent What has happened?
Marianne He's very nervous and, well, he has experienced an involuntary
  transformation, should be temporary.
Vincent That boy is proving much more trouble than I ever thought
  possible. We should take him back with us and bring him up properly.
Marianne You know as well as I do, it's not safe.
Vincent But here he is getting into more and more difficult situations.
Marianne Yes, but at least here he is not hounded by mobs with burning
  torches and pitchforks. He is too used to living here. He wouldn't last
  five minutes in the village.

  Natalia enters with Hayley

Hayley So you must be Valentine's sister?
Natalia I am.
Hayley I'm Hayley.
Marianne I'm Marianne, Valentine's mother, and this is his father
  Vincent.
Hayley Oh, er, pleased to meet you. I didn't realize you'd be joining us?
Marianne Oh, we're not. We are visiting from overseas and just popped
  round to see if Valentine knew of a nice restaurant around here?
Hayley There's a nice Italian down the road, me and Valentine went
  there. The staff are a bit odd, but the food is lovely.
Marianne Italian you say? Maybe. Vincent, shall we?
Vincent We go.

  He exits

Marianne Yes, dear. Lovely to meet you, have a nice evening.
Hayley Thank you, you too.

Marianne leaves

Hayley sits down

Natalia Well have a seat, make yourself at home, Valentine shouldn't
  be long.
Valentine Hayley, I'll be out in a minute. I'm just having a shower.
Hayley Hey baby, not a problem.

Valentine begins to struggle

After a few moments the lights slowly fade to black on the bathroom area

Natalia (*mouthing*) Baby? (*To Hayley*) Would you like a drink?
Hayley Yes please.
Natalia Me too.
Hayley That wine looks good.

*Natalia pours herself a shot of whiskey drinks it then pours Hayley a
glass of wine and hands it to her*

  Thank you. So have you always lived together?
Natalia Yes.
Hayley Are you close?
Natalia Yes.
Hayley Are you joining us for dinner?
Natalia Yes.
Hayley Have you always been this much fun to talk to?

Natalia doesn't reply

  Valentine enters. He is no longer a bat

Valentine Hello.

Hayley gets up and they hug. Natalia rolls her eyes

  You two been getting along?
Hayley Yes, having a great conversation, weren't we?

Natalia Yes ... Would you like some wine, Valentine?

Hayley and Valentine sit

Valentine Yes, please.
Natalia Oh look at that, it's empty. I'll just go into the kitchen and open another bottle.

Natalia exits

Valentine You OK?
Hayley Fine. You could have told me your parents were here?
Valentine I didn't know whether they were coming tonight. I didn't say anything yesterday as I didn't want to scare you, were they OK?
Hayley Your mother was very nice, your dad didn't say much but seemed a bit intense.
Valentine He can be when you first meet him.
Hayley Valentine?
Valentine Yes.
Hayley Is your sister OK?
Valentine She's very protective and not quite used to having visitors.
Hayley That makes sense.
Valentine What'd she say?
Hayley Nothing much, that was the problem. Why you ask?
Valentine No reason ... it's just that we've been living together since, well, forever, and I have a feeling she may get a little jealous. In a nutshell, if she's mean or anything like that, just ignore her. She's not a bad person, it's just that ——
Hayley Don't worry. I'm here to see you, silly, not her. I have a thick skin, I'll just let it run off my back.

Natalia enters with a glass of wine and gives it to Valentine

He drinks, realizes it is blood and downs it in one

Valentine Thank you.
Hayley I thought you didn't drink red wine?
Valentine ... Yes ... but there's a first time for everything. I'm just going to check on the chicken. Natalia, would you give me a hand?
Natalia I'm sure you'll be able to ——
Valentine I really think you should give me a hand!

They move into the kitchen area

Lights go down on Hayley and come up on Valentine and Natalia

Valentine What the hell was that about?
Natalia What?
Valentine Blood in my wine glass!
Natalia Oh I'm sorry, force of habit.
Valentine That's it, we're going out.
Natalia Oh not on account of me I hope.

Lights come up fully

Hayley How's the chicken?
Valentine Ruined. Do you mind if we go out?
Hayley No ... that's fine, but why do I get the feeling this has nothing to
do with the chicken? (*She looks at Natalia*)
Natalia I don't think I like what you're implying?
Hayley That's good because I don't think I like you.
Natalia Feeling's more than mutual.

Valentine begins to usher Hayley out

Valentine OK, going out is suddenly a moment of genius on my part.
See you later, Natalia.
Hayley Terrible meeting you, we really shouldn't do it again
sometime.

Black-out

Scene 17

Hayley's flat. Night

*There are takeaway boxes on the floor and bottles of wine. Hayley and
Valentine are on stage. Valentine is sitting on the sofa, Hayley is standing
— she is rather drunk*

Hayley ... and pale! I mean how pale does she want to be? She looks
like a corpse ... a living, cold, heartless corpse. (*Pause*) Look, I know
she's your sister and everything, but she's nasty and she doesn't like
me ... how can you not like me? ... I mean you like me ... How dare she
... you do like me, don't you?
Valentine Yes, very much.

Hayley sits next to him

Hayley Ah thank you, you're so sweet.

She rests her head on his shoulder. Valentine glances at her neck then looks away, quickly, closing his eyes

Valentine I'm sorry about my sister's behaviour tonight.
Hayley You don't have to apologize for her! Don't get started on her. I mean it, do not get me started on her!
Valentine I won't, but ——
Hayley Good, because once I start I won't stop, seriously.

Pause

Valentine I do apologize, though.
Hayley You're very sweet. (*She falls into Valentine's lap*) I think I may have consumed a little too much alcohol.

Valentine pushes her out of his lap. Long pause. Hayley looks at her wine glass and looks at Valentine

Could you pour me some more wine?

Valentine rises and gets a bottle. He sits down and pours just under half a glass. He stops

Can I have a tiny bit more? ... I'll say when.

Valentine continues to fill the glass. When it is almost at the rim Hayley raises her hand

When.

There is a pause. Hayley drinks then looks at Valentine

You know what?
Valentine What?
Hayley You are absolutely gorgeous.
Valentine (*sitting*) Thank you ... oh ... err, so are you.
Hayley No I'm not.
Valentine Yes you are.
Hayley Ah, you're just saying that.

Valentine No I'm not, you really are very beautiful.
Hayley Ahh, thank you.

Hayley gives Valentine a very big drunken kiss

Valentine You're welcome.
Hayley I'm very drunk ... why aren't you?
Valentine I just haven't drunk very much.
Hayley (*falling on to her knees*) I know that, but why? Why? I want you
   to be drunk ... like me.
Valentine It doesn't matter. I'm having fun.
Hayley Are you though? ... Are you ... really?
Valentine Yes. I like spending time with you.
Hayley I like spending time with you ... too. (*She giggles and stands*)
   Come here.

They kiss

   I want to show you something.
Valentine What's that?
Hayley My bedroom.
Valentine Oh ... I see.
Hayley Come on.
Valentine You're rather drunk.
Hayley That doesn't matter ...

She falls backward. Valentine catches her

   Well, it doesn't normally.
Valentine I think I'd better go.
Hayley No, come into my bedroom ... please.
Valentine I can't, I'm sorry.
Hayley Why not?
Valentine I feel this might be too soon.
Hayley I just want to show you my bedroom.
Valentine Is that all?
Hayley ... Well ... I also want to show you other things in there.
Valentine I don't think we should.

She kisses him

Hayley Are you sure?

Pause. Hayley slaps his bottom

Valentine Yes.

Valentine exits quickly

SCENE 18

Valentine's flat, the living-room. Night

Natalia is sitting down. Valentine storms in and glares at her. He then walks straight across the room and exits

Natalia sits for a while then gets up and follows him. As she exits the lights fade. Valentine enters and hangs upside down. The lights come up on him. Natalia enters

Natalia What are you doing?

Valentine says nothing

Are you sulking?

Valentine is silent

You're sulking aren't you?

Valentine No.

Natalia Valentine, you only ever do this when you're sulking.

Valentine I just want to go to sleep.

Natalia Valentine, you never sleep upside down. You wake up screaming, swearing you're going to fall and break something. You only hang upside down when you're sulking.

Valentine I'm exploring my inner bat!

Natalia You have no inner bat! You have half a bat, which in vampire terms is a bit useless.

Valentine Go away! You do nothing but ridicule me. No wonder I'm not a full vampire, what with your constant heckling!

Natalia Heckling?

Valentine Yes, all the time, anyway I'm not talking to you, not after tonight.

Natalia Tonight, what happened tonight?

Valentine When Hayley was here.

Natalia Oh that.

Valentine You were determined to ruin it from the moment she arrived. That blood stunt is completely unforgivable. Why? Natalia, why do you hate me so much?

Natalia For someone's who's not talking to me you're saying an awful lot.

Valentine Don't avoid the question. Why do you hate me?

Natalia goes to him and holds him as best she can while he's upside down

Natalia I don't hate you, Valentine, quite the opposite in fact. I love you ... very much ... and as your ... sister ... I want to save you any unnecessary hurt.

Valentine But you are hurting me.

Natalia I have to, to save you from the greater hurt.

Valentine tries to get down. He can't

Valentine Erm, little help?

Natalia helps him down

So let me get this straight. To save me hurt, you have to hurt me anyway?

Natalia Yes, but ——

Valentine I know you want to save me from the greater hurt, but what if there is no greater hurt? What if this is the only hurt, this hurt that is supposed to save me from the greater hurt which won't hurt at all because it doesn't exist, so the hurt that is supposed to save me from hurt will actually hurt more because there is no other hurt that I am likely to feel so hurting now is the only hurting I'll be feeling so really this is the greatest hurt though it is a saving type of hurt ——

Natalia What?

Long pause

Valentine What?

Natalia What was all that about?

Valentine I don't know I got lost half way through, but it had something to do with hurt. All I know now though is that my head hurts. Natalia, make it stop.

Natalia It's guilt. You know you're going to have to let Hayley go.

Valentine It's not guilt, it's from hanging upside down.
Natalia Valentine ——
Valentine No Natalia, don't say anything else ... I wish to be ... alone.
Natalia You can't keep avoiding ——
Valentine Uh, I want to be ... alone.
Natalia Look ——
Valentine Go away.
Natalia You gonna hang again?

Long pause

Valentine No.

Black-out

<h2 align="center">SCENE 19</h2>

Hotel room. Night

Vincent and Marianne are sitting on the sofa in silence. There is a long pause

Marianne Hayley seems nice.

Vincent doesn't respond

It'll be good for Valentine to have someone else to talk to. I don't know what all this fuss is about? I mean ——

Vincent looks at Marianne

Vincent What?
Marianne Mm?
Vincent You don't know what all this fuss is about?
Marianne Well, things could be worse.
Vincent Really? Worse? Valentine seeing a mortal, going to Italian restaurants, what could possibly be worse than that?
Marianne No harm was done.
Vincent Yet. That boy is a hazard to himself. No matter what we do he manages to dishonour us!
Marianne Vincent ... listen.

Vincent No, you listen. We are vampires, and as vampires we are expected to carry on the bloodline and what do we have? Him. He has none of the honour or the grandeur of his ancestors. He is an embarrassment to us.

Marianne To you maybe, not me. He is barely a hundred and we knew he would be different. It's a miracle he's here at all.

Vincent A miracle ... Valentine? He's no miracle, he's a disaster! If I had my way he wouldn't have been born.

Marianne If you had any self-control he wouldn't have been.

Vincent This has nothing to do with me, this is all your doing!

Marianne It takes two to ——

Vincent You listen to me. If I had my way and I knew that sorry excuse for a vampire was growing inside you I would have torn him out with my bare hands. When I turned you I was hoping that either he would die or at least be a vampire worthy of our bloodline. I want to take him back with us so that angry mobs will tear him apart and then I will have less to be ashamed of.

Marianne Less? What do you mean?

Vincent My lineage has been soiled by that sack of emotion. He has no powers.

Marianne They will come ... in time.

Vincent And what then? The damage is done! He has been living here so long that he has grown accustomed to the western way of life. He can't be integrated back into the family. He is not fit to be a vampire.

Marianne He is vampire, half-vampire, but soon ——

Vincent No! He is not vampire. That is all that matters at this point. What if this Hayley becomes his wife? Everything we have planned will fall apart.

Marianne By plan you mean all the lies we told him. The web of deceit we managed to weave so effortlessly up to now?

Vincent Indeed a web, a web you helped create.

Marianne I wanted to protect him.

Vincent He shouldn't need protection.

Marianne He's not ready, he needs time.

Vincent He has had one hundred years and now my patience is at an end. This dalliance with a mortal is simply unacceptable.

Marianne What about your dalliance with a mortal?

Vincent says nothing

Me?

Vincent That was a very long time ago.

Marianne Still it happened, and here we are.

Vincent Exactly, look where we are. Here in London clearing up after
our sorry excuse for a son.
Marianne I am sure all will turn out for the best.
Vincent Your naivety is truly astonishing! You are blind when it comes
to your son.
Marianne A parent's love is unconditional.
Vincent As is a vampire's hatred.

Lights fade to black-out

SCENE 20

Valentine's flat, the living-room. Day

*The curtains are drawn. Hayley and Valentine are lying on the sofa
watching a horror movie*

Hayley Are you sure she's asleep?
Valentine Yes.

Pause

Hayley Are you quite sure?
Valentine I'm very sure.

Pause

Hayley Cool ... does she always sleep during the day?
Valentine ... Oh ... yeah ... she works ... nights.
Hayley That figures ... What is she, a prostitute? (*Pause*) Sorry.
Valentine Waitress ...
Hayley Ah, OK.

Long pause

Ooooh, that's gross.
Valentine Mmm, I guess so, but you see what they're ... well, yeah it is.
Hayley Why are we watching this again?
Valentine Shall I switch it off?
Hayley Oh yeah.

He switches off the film with a remote

So, what shall we do now?

Valentine ... Shall we talk?

Hayley Talk, yeah, that's good. That is good, right, it's just talk, not that we should talk.

Valentine No, just talk.

Hayley OK good.

Valentine Well when they were shooting the movie we were watching, the weather ——

Hayley (*putting her fingers to his lips*) No.

Valentine Well ... oh ... what are your plans tomorrow?

Hayley Erm ... I'm seeing you tomorrow ... I am, right?

Valentine Oh yes, you are, yes.

Hayley Sorry I just get very nervous.

Long pause. Valentine looks at Hayley, she looks at him they smile and look front. Hayley looks at Valentine, he looks at her they smile. Hayley rests her head on his shoulder, he rests his head, they turn their heads and kiss. They start kissing passionately. Hayley begins to unbutton Valentine's shirt, Valentine goes to remove Hayley's top

Black-out

CURTAIN

ACT II

Scene 1

Valentine's flat, the living-room. Night

Hayley is asleep on the sofa. She is wrapped in a sheet. Valentine is kneeling on the floor in boxer shorts. Lights fade up, creepy music begins to play and Valentine looks up. His face is contorted almost like a disgruntled dog. He leaps to his feet, his body is tense and he begins to snarl. He walks around menacingly. The music stops suddenly and Valentine becomes his normal self

Valentine Oh ... I'm doing that. I'm actually OK; I'm still me, no involuntary drooling.

Valentine goes over to Hayley and kneels beside her, sniffs and closes his eyes, then opens them

(*Walking away*) No uncontrollable bloodlust. I'm fine, which is ... fine. No, better than fine, it's great! (*He sits on the end of the sofa*) I'm OK, I've made love and I'm OK!

Hayley wakes, crawls up behind him and puts her arms around him

Hayley Of course you're OK.
Valentine I know, it's just a little surprising that's all.
Hayley Surprising? Why?
Valentine No reason ... just, well ... (*he gets up*) ... yeah.
Hayley What?
Valentine I'm sorry, what?
Hayley You didn't finish your sentence ... you just kind of trailed off.
Valentine Yes I did, didn't I?
Hayley (*confused*) OK.

Pause

What's the time?
Valentine (*looking at his watch*) Just after nine.

Hayley (*getting up*) Wow! (*She giggles*) We've been asleep for a while.

She brings him to sit. Pause

Will she be at work now?
Valentine Who?
Hayley Your sister?
Valentine Mmm, I'm sure she's out and about.
Hayley (*seductively*) Well, what shall we do now?
Valentine We could watch a film.
Hayley A film?
Valentine Yeah.
Hayley From your collection?
Valentine Well ... yeah.
Hayley Well as much as I like you and can appreciate your taste in films, I'd rather not sit through another video nasty right now, and you don't seem like the kind of guy to have a trashy romantic comedy tucked away.
Valentine But I have *Dating Dracula's Daughter*!
Hayley Er no, I don't think so ...
Valentine Well there may be something. How about *Dracula Goes to Camp* — sound good?
Hayley Yeah ... Let's not watch a movie. Hey Valentine?
Valentine Mm?
Hayley Come here!

She drags him back into the sofa and they kiss

Lights fade to black

SCENE 2

Valentine's flat, the kitchen. Early morning

Hayley enters, scrambling for a light switch. She finds it and puts the light on. Natalia is sitting at the table, knitting

Natalia Good-evening.
Hayley Oh ... hello, I guess.
Natalia I fear we may have gotten off on the wrong foot.
Hayley No! Really? I thought we had a real connection, proper friend stuff ... you know.

Natalia Sarcasm doesn't suit you.

Hayley And being friendly doesn't suit you.

Pause

Natalia I don't like you.

Hayley Well d'uh!

Natalia And you don't like me.

Hayley Your powers of deduction are truly incredible!

Natalia Yes, well, my poor misguided little brother has taken quite a shine to you. So, as much as it pains me to say it, we should try and get along for his sake if nothing else.

Hayley Or we could just avoid each other, which works better for me. I find it hard to get along with cold-hearted people, especially when I know they don't like me.

Natalia Listen, Harry ——

Hayley It's Hayley!

Natalia Whatever ... You really should learn to think before you speak, because what may sound like a great, scathing put-down in your pretty little head doesn't always work when you come to say it out loud. Also trying to avoid each other won't work. Judging by your attire this isn't a flying visit. Also, in case you haven't noticed, this isn't exactly a castle, and if you're planning to continue to come here, which is likely considering my brother's ... condition, we are bound to bump into each other, seeing as I have no east wing to retreat to until you're gone.

Hayley That's the first time I've heard a relationship referred to as a condition. Now listen, you heartless ——

Natalia Ssssh! Remember think first ... then speak.

Hayley OK ... I have spent the entire day in bed with your baby brother! He is now waiting for me to return with a glass of water. Also after the day I've had I think your brother is neither poor nor misguided. As for thinking and speaking, I believe actions speak louder than words. Now if you don't mind, I'm going to get some more ... action.

Natalia So you're the screamer! And here I was hoping he was killing you.

Hayley Wha —— you mean you ... just sat here and list —— you ... what are you, a pervert?

Natalia I was just innocently sitting here.

Hayley Innocently?

Natalia Yes.

Hayley In the dark? Sounds like we have a seasoned voyeur on our hands?

Natalia You sure you know what that big word means?

Hayley What are you implying?
Natalia Nothing.

Long pause

  Not much anyway.
Hayley Now look you ——

Valentine enters

Valentine Hayley ... oh, hello, Natalia.
Natalia Hello, brother dear. I was just chatting to Harry.
Both Hayley!
Natalia Oooh stereo! Heard you've been having fun. In fact I heard everything.
Hayley She was spying.
Natalia Without intent. Anyway, unless you kids need me for anything I'm going out.
Hayley What now? What type of restaurant do you work at? You sure you're not a prostitute?
Natalia What ——

Valentine pushes Natalia out the door

  Natalia exits

Valentine Bye, Natalia, see you later.
Hayley So.

Valentine walks over to her

Valentine So.
Hayley Water? (*She hands him a glass of water*)

Valentine drinks half of it, and hands back the glass

Valentine Thank you.

Black-out

SCENE 3

Valentine's flat, the kitchen. The following evening

Valentine is seated at the table. There are two empty blood bottles in front of him. Natalia enters, notices the bottles and sits opposite him

Natalia I take it she's left, seeing as you are not trying to suppress your true appetite.

Valentine Yes she's left.

Long pause. Valentine smiles at her

Natalia How long are you going to keep this up?

Valentine What?

Natalia What you think, stud?

Valentine Look, Natalia?

Natalia What on earth do you think you're doing?

Valentine It's OK, we used protection, and as you can see I'm still regular me, all is fine.

Natalia Fine? Do you not realize the risks involved? What if she became a vampire, what would you do then?

Valentine We use protection.

Natalia Look, things may go wrong, remember, heightened sexual powers.

Valentine Really?

Natalia Of course.

Valentine Vampirism is so cool!

Natalia What if it split?

Valentine They ... they do that?

Natalia Yes they do.

Valentine Well I don't think any of them did.

Natalia Maybe not, but I wouldn't leave it to chance. She won't make a loyal vampire.

Valentine What do you mean loyal?

Natalia She's young, feisty. If you turn her into a vampire she'll leave you.

Valentine She wouldn't leave me.

Natalia She will. Granted she'll return after a few decades. Remember she'll be immortal so once all her mortal friends grow old and suffer and cease to be, she'll return to her old flame Valentine who forced her to watch all her friends die. I'm sure you'll agree that's not quite romantic is it? Leave her, Valentine.

Valentine But ——

Natalia But what? There's no choice anymore, this is the eventuality. If you break up with her now, you lose her, but you save her from a terrible ordeal. She was born mortal ... you can't make her a vampire, it's not fair.

Valentine I don't want to make her a vampire.

Natalia That's out of your hands now you are sleeping together.

Valentine I know. I know, but it's not that simple.

Natalia Of course it is, you meet and say it's over. There job done.

Valentine I know...

Natalia Then you also know what you have to do?

Valentine I'm seeing her tomorrow. I'll do it then.

Natalia Good boy.

Valentine looks forlorn. Natalia hugs him

Lights fade to black-out

SCENE 4

Hayley's flat. Night

Hayley and Valentine are watching a movie together. Hayley is struggling to stay awake

Hayley I'm so sleepy, baby, do you mind if I take a nap?

Valentine No, no course not. I'm just going to get some water.

Valentine exits

Hayley gets comfortable and falls asleep

Valentine enters with water and sets it down on the table. He looks towards Hayley. He walks round and kneels by her making sure she's asleep. He stands up

(*Whispering*) Hayley? Hayley? ... You asleep Hayley? ... Are you? ... You sleeping, Hayley?

Hayley doesn't respond

OK, right then, right, right then, OK, right ... OK ...

Valentine starts taking deep breaths

OK, Hayley I ...

He breaks away, starts taking deep breaths again. He stops suddenly

Who'd think this would be so difficult? She's asleep for God's sake!
OK, Hayley ... I know you're asleep, but I also know that you're
a light sleeper, I have the bruises on my shins to prove it. So I'm
assuming that what I'm about to say will fall into your subconscious
and therefore you will remember it.

Long pause

Hayley, I can't see you anymore. I really like you and your company,
but ... well there isn't really a but. I just can't continue seeing you. I
haven't been entirely honest with you, I wanted to be, I really did, but
if you knew, one you wouldn't believe me and two ... well I can't think
of a two right now, but there would definitely be a two and quite likely
a three, a four, a five, a six ... you get the idea. Fact of the matter is, if
I continue seeing you, bad things will happen to you ... and me quite
possibly, but you're the one I worry about hurting. I'm a bad person ...
not intentionally, it's kind of hereditary. It's not you, it's my ... family
bloodline. I want to be with you and everything that comes with it, but
I can't.

Valentine walks away from Hayley and talks softly to himself

To be honest, strictly speaking I shouldn't want that at all. Frankly I
should have eaten you by now. Of course I'd never do that. Not at the
moment anyway, but the problem is that at some point down the line ...
I probably will ... There's too many risks involved, all with very nasty
consequences. I probably should have ended it earlier ... then again,
I probably should never have even started seeing you. As always my
family are right. All their arguments against us had valid points, I just
didn't want to listen and now we've come so far, it's too dangerous for
us to carry on.

*He walks back over to Hayley, kisses her gently on the forehead. She
murmurs and moves slightly*

Goodbye, Hayley.

Black-out

SCENE 5

Valentine's flat, the living-room. Early afternoon

Marianne and Valentine are sitting together watching TV. Valentine is resting his head on Marianne's lap

Marianne How are you feeling?
Valentine Yeah well ... Mmmph.
Marianne I know it doesn't seem it now but it is for the best.
Valentine (*sitting up*) Is it, really?
Marianne In the grand scheme of things, yes.
Valentine Grand scheme? What grand scheme?
Marianne When you become a full vampire ——
Valentine Exactly, when? When will it happen? My hundredth birthday? Been and gone. The day of my promotion as it were is a bit like the end of the world, lots of different dates but nothing ever happens!
Marianne I know it's frustrating but you are special.
Valentine (*standing*) Cursed more like it, doomed to rot away, on this planet alone ... The thought of immortality is beginning to depress me. I mean, how can it be perceived as a good thing?
Marianne Think of all you'll see that others can only dream of.

Pause

Valentine Nope ... still depressed.
Marianne I know it's hard to believe at the moment but this can be seen as a gift. Before long you may appreciate it.
Valentine Appreciate it? I'm going to be alone forever, I hypnotize myself, I can't bring myself to drink blood from the living which is essential to keep me ... err ... alive, I turn into some bizarre literal batman when I'm nervous rather than your everyday multi-purpose bat, hanging upside down gives me a headache and I sleep in a coffin which scares me to death ... which is fitting seeing that technically I am dead! Gift? Some gift! (*He sits*)
Marianne Things will get better. Once you ——
Valentine (*standing*) Here we go again, once I become a full vampire. What? All will be fine? I've been waiting for centuries ... literally, and to be honest I'm not sure I want to be a vampire anymore.

Natalia and Vincent enter

They have been listening

Natalia All this coming from the one who said vampirism was cool.

Valentine (*sitting down*) That was different; I was with Hayley then, finally felt good about myself for a change. I wasn't so damned ... lonely!

Vincent Lonely? Lonely? You felt good when you were with her, a mortal? Sometimes Valentine I ——

Marianne Vincent ... please, not now.

Vincent shoots a look at Marianne and, angry, exits. After a pause Marianne follows him

After a moment the doorbell rings. Valentine and Natalia look at each other. Long pause

Slowly Valentine gets up and exits

Natalia watches him leave

Hayley bursts in

Valentine (*off*) Hello?

Natalia Oh hello, Harry.

Hayley Quiet, you!

Valentine enters

Hayley Why haven't you been returning my calls? I thought you were coming over today? What the hell happened?

Valentine Well, I thought I should give you some space, seeing as we broke up.

Hayley What? We ... we broke up? ... Were you planning to tell me or was I just supposed to guess?

Valentine I did tell you, last night.

Hayley When? I don't remember that!

Pause. Hayley looks at Natalia who is giggling

Would you please ask Morticia to leave?

Natalia Oh no, I want to stay, after all, I think Valentine would want me here, isn't that right Valentine? Anyway, break-ups can be so traumatic and after all we've shared between us — how did you put it? — proper friend stuff? I wouldn't miss this for the world.

Hayley Figures, seeing as this is what you wanted all along. Which is why I want to know whether your decision Valentine, was an independent one?

Natalia He decided it was for the best.

Hayley After you told him it would be, I bet?

Natalia He took it upon himself.

Valentine It is for the best ... in the long run.

Hayley Why ... what happened, did I do something?

Valentine No, it's just that ——

Hayley Whoah ... hang on! I still don't even remember you dumping me.

Valentine It was last night.

Hayley All I remember is watching a film and then I fell asleep.

Very long pause. Hayley looks at Valentine

No you didn't?

Valentine nods

You told me while I was asleep?

Natalia sniggers

Look, are you going to leave, or am I going to have to make you.

Valentine nods at Natalia

Natalia But it's just getting interesting. I like the way her face screws up when she's angry, imagine having to endure that temper day in, day out. It'd be like living next to a volcano. Also, just between you and me, friends ... as we are, the screwed-up face thing ... not a good look for you, then again neither was the half-naked thing, or that hideous thing you wore on our first meeting. Then again some people don't look good until their twilight years. But I don't think that'll work for you either, oh listen to me kicking you while you're down, I'm such a bitch.

Hayley You said it!

Natalia But at least I have the intelligence and looks to keep people interested.

Hayley Like who? Valentine? Isn't that a little sick? Then again you don't look well, all pale and pasty, what is it with you?

Valentine I think you'd better leave, Natalia.

Natalia Aw! Oh well OK, but she'd better be gone when I get back!
Bye, Harry.
Hayley For the last time it's Hayley. H.A. ——
Natalia Whatever.

Natalia exits

Hayley God I hate her! Then again you're not much better, dumping me
in my sleep ... my sleep! What on earth were you thinking?
Valentine Well you're a light sleeper, I thought that maybe ——
Hayley Maybe what? I was asleep for Christ's sake! How am I going
to hear you?
Valentine I thought ——
Hayley Well you thought wrong. Being dumped by text message was
bad, but this, well ... we have a new champion. Talk about cowardice.
Am I that scary? Well ... am I?
Valentine A little.
Hayley Well don't you think I have the right, considering the
circumstances?
Valentine I guess.
Hayley Guess! You guess. I don't believe you! Course I have the right, one
you dump me in my sleep, then two you just leave, no note, nothing.
Valentine I didn't leave a note because I told you ——
Hayley No you didn't, listen very carefully because you seem to keep
forgetting, I ... was ... asleep, in bed, not conscious, you could have
said whatever you liked, I wouldn't have heard you. It's ridiculous
you even contemplated I'd hear what you were saying but no ... you
assumed I did!
Valentine I'm sorry, but ——
Hayley Why? ... (*She looks around*) And why is it always so dark in
here?
Valentine What?
Hayley Never mind ... Why did you break up with me? Seeing as I'm
awake now, do you think you could do me the common courtesy of
telling me why you left me? (*She sits*)
Valentine It's just that soon ... things are bound to get a little complicated.
(*He sits*)
Hayley What? Why?
Valentine I can't explain ——
Hayley I think you should try.
Valentine You wouldn't believe me if I told you.
Hayley Trust me I wouldn't put anything past you now ... so spill!
Valentine I can't, I'm sorry but I really can't. I don't want to change
things.

Hayley And dumping me hasn't?

Valentine I'm not what you think I am.

Hayley (*standing*) This isn't making any sense. The least you can do is tell me why us being together is such a problem? I've put up with a lot from you, the nervousness, the hay fever, the film collection ... the mega bitch of a sister, I've put a hell of a lot of work into you and I think I deserve a little more than this crap you're feeding me!

Valentine I'm a v ... a v ...

Hayley Vegan? What does that have to do with anything? Plenty of vegans and non-vegans have happy and uncomplicated relationships, that is without a doubt the worst excuse I have ever heard! If you don't like me just ——

Valentine I'm not vegan.

Hayley What the hell is it then?

Valentine I'm a vampire!

Very long pause. Hayley is a little taken aback. Valentine looks sheepish

Hayley You know, vegan ... would have been slightly more convincing.

Valentine I told you, you wouldn't believe me.

Hayley Well yeah, neither would anyone else!

Valentine It's true.

Hayley You mean you belong to one of those weird cults, oh God, you don't go around slitting your wrists with razor blades and asking confused and lonely teenagers to drink from you, do you?

Valentine No I'm a fully-fledged, living ... dead vampire.

Hayley Again, the cult thing would have been more convincing.

Valentine But it's not the truth.

Hayley The truth! That's all I want and what you give me is ludicrous excuses, if you don't want to be with me just tell me ... why?

Valentine I have told you why.

Hayley You seriously don't expect me to accept "I'm a vampire" as a reason do you?

Valentine Think about it, Hayley, the garlic bread, why it's so dark in here? ... Natalia, being so pale? It all adds up.

Hayley Why are you lying to me? It just makes the situation worse.

Valentine If we continued as we were the situation would've become much worse.

Hayley You are not a vampire. Surely if you were I'd be one too by now.

Valentine We used protection.

Hayley Look, there are no such things as vampires!

Pause

Natalia (*off*) Has she gone yet?
Hayley No, I haven't.
Natalia (*off*) Can I get you anything, tea, coffee ... chloroform?
Valentine Go away, Natalia.

Natalia laughs

Valentine Natalia!
Natalia (*off*) OK, OK, I'm going.
Hayley (*sitting*) I think I was beginning to fall for you.

Long pause

Why are you breaking up with me?
Valentine I don't want to risk hurting you.
Hayley But I'm hurting now.
Valentine (*standing*) I'm talking about a hurt that you couldn't possibly bear.
Hayley You're redirecting me to the claim that you're a vampire, aren't you? (*Standing*) Look, anything would be a lot better than that. You're not ready for a commitment, you don't feel the same way, I'd even be happy if you told me you were gay! (*Slight pause*) You're not gay are you?
Valentine What? No!
Hayley We always have to check, you're absolutely sure? It's OK if you are, I'll understand.
Valentine No, Hayley, I am not gay!
Hayley Right ... OK. (*Long pause*) You could have lied, you know, made it easier on me?
Valentine OK ... Hayley, I'm gay.
Hayley Well it's not gonna work now!
Valentine (*sitting*) Oh yeah, guess not. Sorry.
Hayley Not as sorry as I am. Why is it every time I think I'm happy and in an intimate, reciprocated relationship, I always get pulled up short?
Valentine I'm very sorry.
Hayley Stop saying that! If you're really sorry you'd see how much I'm hurting and make it stop. You made a decision, but as always in these situations you can't justify it. You say you're sorry, I'll go home and assume I'm fine, then tomorrow everything will run through my head, our first date, the first kiss, your eyes, your body, and the first

time we made love. (*Sitting*) Do you know what that's like? I will
have imaginary conversations, what I could say to win you back. (*She
touches him and stands*) Next I'll be yelling insults because you broke
up with me. Why do I never see it coming? What am I doing wrong?
I get all hopeful and then it ends. If you're not asleep at the time or
told in a text message you can only tell if you're going to break up
moments before it happens. It's never immediate, you'll meet, they'll
behave as normal, they'll find a quiet spot, sit you down (*she sits*)
then you see it. It's all in their eyes, and you know the words before
they come. "You're a lovely girl, but ..." Sometimes you can tell long
before the actual break-up. The daily phone calls stop, the regular text
messages dry up. That is it, you may not want to admit it, but you
know in yourself it's over. That is slightly easier to deal with, but this,
Valentine, this is one of those that take months to get over. In a couple
of weeks I'll think I have moved on but every now and then I'll see
something ... a couple kissing ... that'll set it all off. I'll remember
everything that was said to me, all those lovely words I believed,
because I wanted to, that now mean nothing at all, and the hurt starts
all over again.
Valentine I ... don't know what to say.
Hayley There is something you can say ... but you're not going to are
you?

Valentine says nothing

I can't be here now. I'm going.
Valentine I'm telling the truth, Hayley.
Hayley I wish you were, Valentine.

She exits

Natalia enters; she's really bouncy

Natalia So how is she?

Marianne enters

Marianne Natalia! Please.

Affronted, Natalia exits

Valentine?
Valentine I've really hurt her.

Marianne She'll be all right.

Valentine I didn't think this would happen. I mean look at you and Dad, you were mortal when you met.

Marianne Like I said, it was a very long time ago and a very different time.

Valentine Why?

Marianne What?

Valentine Why, why was it so different what happened?

Marianne The eyes, all I remember is those eyes. I couldn't break away from that stare. I had met him for all of ten minutes and looking into those eyes I knew I was his. From that moment nothing would stop me loving this man. He was not someone I would have even considered in a romantic capacity but ... well, now I know what it was, but then, back then, I was young, naïve. I thought I was going to take a year to see the world, in those eyes however I saw the truth — I was running, running away from myself, who I was, who I was becoming, who everyone expected me to be. In those eyes I saw something, something wild, and something new, something I wanted. I had escaped and he was my freedom. All that wanting had to show itself, and soon I fell pregnant. And then it happened. All I felt was pain followed by a feeling of release, he had bitten me before but not like this, this was savage, uncontrolled. I passed out and when I awoke I saw him sitting at the end of the bed. I rose and approached the dresser. I had no reflection. He whispered in my ear, I don't know what he said to me and it didn't matter, I had already forgiven him, he had saved me from everything I was running from and I loved him for that and always will. I think deep down he sees himself in you and he fears for you. He knows too well what might happen if, like him, you lose control and so do I.

Valentine Yes ... well, Hayley and I are over now and I'm sure you're both very happy.

Marianne Don't be silly, I hate seeing you like this.

Valentine And Dad?

Marianne Well I'm sure he'll have some sympathy for you. Come on, let's see if we can find him.

Valentine No, I'm too depressed to stand.

Marianne Valentine, don't be silly, come on.

Reluctantly Valentine gets up

Valentine and Marianne exit

As they exit, lights fade

SCENE 6

Valentine's flat, the kitchen. Night

Vincent is nuzzling Natalia's neck and then drinks from her wrist. There are bottles of blood on the table, some is spilt and Natalia has blood smeared around her mouth

Valentine and Marianne enter. Vincent and Natalia don't notice. When they do, they very calmly break apart. Valentine is dumbfounded

Vincent Natalia, take Valentine into the next room, but tell him nothing.
Valentine What? No!
Marianne I think that is best, Valentine ... for now
Valentine But ——
Marianne Please, Valentine, I can't explain this, not now.

Natalia goes to grab Valentine's arm

Valentine Don't touch me!
Vincent Go!

Valentine exits

Natalia looks at Vincent. They kiss

Natalia exits

Marianne and Vincent stare at each other for a moment

Vincent So?
Marianne Why?
Vincent Is that all? Why? Well I didn't expect that. That is not a normal response just one calm "Why?" Then again you never were a normal girl.
Marianne You look different.
Vincent What?
Marianne Your eyes, they seem different to me.
Vincent What are you talking about?
Marianne I haven't seen this before, there is a distance.
Vincent You haven't seen because you haven't looked, not really, not like you used to. That is why. You have been blind to all that has happened between us. This was inevitable.

Marianne I ... I forgive ——
Vincent No! I don't want forgiveness, I am not sorry, I have never been
  sorry, I am ashamed, but not sorry.
Marianne Ashamed? Of Valentine?
Vincent Yes.

Pause

  And of you. I have lived with you and Valentine, tarnishing my
  reputation, my family name. Everything I once stood for has been
  taken away by you and your pathetic son. All these years, these
  decades spent with you, that shame I felt, began to grow and soon,
  every time I looked at you, all I saw was a mistake that I was paying
  for every day.
Marianne How long have you felt like this?
Vincent That is of no relevance.
Marianne How long?
Vincent Since him.
Marianne What? That was at ——
Vincent Exactly.
Marianne Why spend decades with me then?
Vincent It seemed easier. But monogamy and faithfulness to one,
  especially a former mortal, is not something I ever planned for myself.
  I need a companion who is a real vampire, no remnants of human
  emotion, no ties to their offspring.
Marianne So you chose Natalia? But our plan?
Vincent Ah yes, our plan. Did you really believe I was going to let
  someone like Natalia end up with a simpleton like Valentine? Did
  you?
Marianne But we ——
Vincent But we what? Yes, we said that Natalia would live with
  Valentine until he became a proper vampire, then they would return
  and carry on my legacy.
Marianne Yes.
Vincent No! Natalia knew that she would be mine. Did you not think it
  strange she was happy to protect that imbecile Valentine? I promised
  her myself, my family name and all that accompanies it. Not a bad fee
  for babysitting wouldn't you agree?
Marianne I ——
Vincent You really had no idea?
Marianne Did you ever feel anything for me? Ever?

Long pause

Vincent No.

Marianne I love you.

Vincent I know.

Marianne Does that mean nothing to you?

Vincent Why should it?

Marianne The time we spent when we first met?

Vincent You were just another lost girl I spotted while I was peckish.

Marianne But we have spent lifetimes together?

Vincent Granted, that was not convenient. But my plan, though long in execution, has now come to fruition.

Marianne But what of me? You made me vampire.

Vincent An oversight.

Marianne You can't just leave me?

Vincent Of course I can. We have been together for far too long and now after decades of patience and cleaning up after the black spot in my lineage, I am to have a companion worthy of my name. Now I think it is time to execute the second part of the plan, don't you? (*Calling off*) Natalia, Valentine will you come in here?

Natalia and Vincent both enter

Natalia stands next to Vincent

Vincent Valentine, your mother has something to tell you.

Marianne Vincent, I can't.

Vincent Of course you can, the time has come to break that web of deceit.

Valentine Mother, what is he talking about?

Vincent Yes, Marianne, whatever am I talking about?

Marianne Valentine, when you were born we decided once you were slightly older we would send you away. Because you were half-human you would be vulnerable to the angry mobs and scared villagers and it would be difficult to keep you safe. We decided you would need a companion and it was decided Natalia would accompany you.

Valentine My sister. Look, I know all this.

Marianne Valentine ... Natalia is not your sister. We have been lying to you.

Valentine I don't understand.

Vincent It is quite simple. She was sent here to look after you, knowing that once you became a full vampire she would come back and become my companion. Now though, since you are a very late bloomer, we decided to skip a step. Now the truth is out. (*He approaches Marianne*) Now ... I go.

He exits

Natalia goes to follow

Valentine Natalia?

Natalia looks back, then exits

Marianne Valentine ... I ...
Valentine You knew?
Marianne What?
Valentine You knew for all this time and never told me. You have been lying to me since birth?
Marianne It was for your own protection.
Valentine Since birth!
Marianne I didn't know this was going to happen. He told me that we would make Natalia a gift.
Valentine Gift?
Marianne When you became full vampire, she would have been your companion. I am truly sorry, Valentine, you were not supposed to find out like this.
Valentine I have to go.
Marianne No, Valentine ... please, we need to talk about this.
Valentine It's too late.
Marianne Valentine! Where are you going?

Valentine exits

Hayley (*off*) Hey, the door was open, I passed your dad and sister. Don't people overseas close doors? Look, I came to apologize ... are you crying? ... Valentine, where are you going? Valentine?
Marianne Let him go.

Hayley enters

Hayley What's going on?
Marianne I think it best if you took a seat.

Hayley sits and looks at the table

Hayley Is that blood?
Marianne Yes.
Hayley Oh.

Pause

Why is there blood on the kitchen table?

Marianne It's a long story.

Hayley OK, look, I saw Her Royal Bitchiness and Mr Intense striding down the road arm-in-arm, I come in the open door to be greeted by Valentine with tears in his eyes heading out that same door and now I am sitting at a blood-stained table. Also, at the risk of sounding rude, you are not exactly the picture of a happy mother. So correct me if I'm wrong but my guess is some serious shit has just hit the fan, am I right?

Marianne Well yes. My partner of, well, far too many years for you to understand has left me for someone else. I knew deep down he was bored of me, but I didn't want to admit it. I also had to tell my son I had been lying to him all his life. Everything has crashed down around me and I am alone and quite frankly frightened.

Hayley Hey, hey, come here, sit down. Who did Mr Intense run off with? Oh no. That ... hang on, isn't that incest? She's Valentine's sister for crying out loud!

Marianne No ... no she's not.

Hayley Well who the hell is she then?

Marianne When we sent Valentine here for his own protection we sent Natalia to keep an eye on him, to be his companion. We told Valentine she was his sister at the time. It seemed the best thing to do.

Hayley Mmm, that is quite a lie.

Marianne I have been so blind. I thought that once Valentine became a full vampire he would come back with Natalia and we would be a proper family.

Hayley Full vampire? Listen, you are not vampires.

Marianne stands in front of Hayley and opens her mouth

Any dentist can do that kind of work.

Marianne shows her eyes, which swirl, to Hayley

That not so much. But come on ... vampires?

Marianne picks up one of the blood bottles and drinks it

Hayley Ewww! But that might just be juice.

Marianne Look.

She takes out a mirror and stands behind Hayley. She hands her the mirror. After much double checking Hayley puts the mirror on the table

Hayley How do you do that? You're there but you weren't in the mirror ... so the blood ... and the teeth ... you're a vampire.
Marianne I am.
Hayley You're not going to kill me are you?
Marianne Not today, no.
Hayley So is Mr Intense a vampire?
Marianne Yes.
Hayley And —— ?
Marianne Mm hm.

Pause

Hayley Valentine? Oh my God I slept with a vampire!
Marianne Half-vampire.
Hayley Am I?
Marianne I'm not sure.

Panicking, Hayley picks up the mirror and upon seeing herself, is relieved. She still checks her teeth though

Hayley So Valentine was telling the truth?
Marianne He was.
Hayley This is all so weird.
Marianne Would you like some tea?
Hayley Will that make it any less weird? Why is it people seem to think tea will solve everything? Your partner has run out on you, my boyfriend has turned out to be a vampire, but let's put this in perspective over tea.
Marianne Tea?
Hayley Yes please.

During the following exchange Marianne makes tea. Once made she puts it on the table and sits opposite Hayley

Vampires? You are sure.

Marianne opens her mouth

Hayley OK ... wow! Why, whenever I meet someone, is it never simple? I meet the perfect cute, sweet guy and he turns out to be a monster.
Marianne Valentine is not a monster. Surely you know that?
Hayley But he will be, right?
Marianne Not necessarily. Valentine was conceived while I was mortal. Granted I was turned while pregnant and normally that would kill the

child, but not Valentine, and now he is half-human, a hybrid, possibly permanently.

Hayley Permanently? You mean he'll be half and half forever?

Marianne It's possible, he has lived a hundred years with no change.

Hayley Whoah, whoah, whoah, he's a hundred?

Marianne Yes.

Hayley One-zero-zero?

Marianne Yes.

Hayley He doesn't look it.

Marianne He's a vampire.

Hayley Oh right, course ... sorry. So maybe we could get back together. OK there's an age gap, but nobody would know. Also if he goes all vampire maybe it could work. I mean you seem perfectly nice, and he is your son. What do you think?

Pause

Marianne Do you love him?

Hayley Yes.

Marianne Then it will work.

Hayley Thank you.

Marianne Now let's find him and tell him.

Hayley What, now?

Marianne Trust me, now is the perfect time.

They exit

Lights fade as they exit

SCENE 7

The florist shop. Night

Vincent and Natalia are onstage. Valentine enters and stops dead

Valentine How did you —— ?

Natalia dangles the keys from her fingers

Vincent I thought I'd see what you've been spending your inheritance on. A flower shop! Really, Valentine. Anyway, it doesn't matter now, seeing as I'm cutting you off.

Valentine What?

Vincent I am cutting my ties, cleansing my name. Cleaning the slate and you are no longer my concern.

Valentine But you can't cut my inheritance, I'm your son.

Vincent My son? Not any more. Let me be clear, Valentine, I have never loved you. Ever since your birth you have been nothing but a burden. Now you are a hundred and I refuse to spend any more money or time cradling you. Which reminds me, your delightful little apartment?

Valentine ...

Natalia Your flat.

Valentine Oh.

Vincent On the market in a week's time.

Valentine You can't do this. I'll be homeless.

Vincent Well, there is another option.

Valentine What?

Vincent I could tear out your lungs and leave you here to see your first and last sunrise.

Valentine I don't know what to say ...

Vincent Well say something!! How did I create such a pathetic, incoherent sorry little excuse for a life? I should have killed you long ago. I will never understand why I didn't? Then these past hundred years would never have been so humiliating. You shame me. Every day you exist my name is dragged further into the mud. From this moment on, you are nothing to me. I will no longer acknowledge your existence. Any link you have to me will be severed. I will let you live, but unsupported here in London. Any attempt to see or contact me will result in death for you and your mother. She is all you have now, Valentine. There is nothing else.

Valentine Natalia, please, you are all I have known. Please, you must feel something for me?

Natalia In the beginning maybe, but this was my destiny. Valentine, you were a detour, granted a lengthy one, but still just a detour.

Vincent She was your babysitter.

Valentine Natalia?

She walks over and kisses Valentine on the forehead. She begins to leave, then turns back

Natalia Goodbye, Valentine ... it has been ... emotional.

Natalia exits

Vincent We leave now. Just remember I wish you never existed and from this moment on you don't! But I think you should have something to remember me by.

Vincent viciously attacks Valentine

As Vincent exits he looks back at Valentine bloodied and crumpled on the floor and sneers. He exits

Valentine begins to cry

A few moments later Hayley and Marianne appear

Hayley Oh God, Valentine!

She runs to him. They embrace

Should we call an ambulance?
Marianne He will heal.

Long pause. Marianne goes over to them and kneels behind them

We all will.

Black-out

CURTAIN

FURNITURE AND PROPERTY LIST

ACT I

SCENE 1

On stage: VALENTINE'S LIVING-ROOM/ HAYLEY'S FLAT/ HOTEL ROOM
Sofa
Telephone
Remote control
Knitting
Bottle of blood

VALENTINE'S KITCHEN/ FLORIST SHOP/ RESTAURANT
Table (to act as counter in florist shop)
Chairs
Tea things

SCENE 2

Strike: Knitting
Bottle of blood

Off stage: Bottle of blood (**Natalia**)

SCENE 3

On stage: As before

SCENE 4

Set: Notebook
Pen

SCENE 5

Set: Knitting

SCENE 6

Strike: Knitting

Off stage: Pack of tissues, bouquet (**Valentine**)

SCENE 7

On stage: As before

SCENE 8

Set: Candle, menus

SCENE 9

On stage: As before

Off stage: Suitcase, large black hold-all containing gas mask (**Marianne**)

SCENE 10

Set: Two half-filled wine glasses
                Bottle of wine

Off stage: Gas mask, plate of garlic bread (**Vincent**)
                Plate of mushrooms (**Vincent**)

SCENE 11

Strike: Candle
                Menus
                Glasses
                Bottle of wine
                Plates

SCENE 12

On stage: As before

Off stage: Gas mask (**Vincent**)

SCENE 13

On stage: As before

SCENE 14

On stage: As before

SCENE 15

On stage:	As before

SCENE 16

Set:	Side table. On it: Bottle of wine, glasses, bottle of whisky, glass
Off stage:	Glass of blood (**Natalia**)
Personal:	Pipe (**Valentine**)

SCENE 17

Strike:	Table Glasses Whisky
Set:	Takeaway boxes Wine bottles

SCENE 18

Strike:	Takeaway boxes Wine bottles

SCENE 19

On stage:	As before

SCENE 20

On stage:	As before

ACT II

SCENE 1

Set:	Sheet

SCENE 2

Strike:	Sheet
Set:	Knitting Glass of water

SCENE 3

Strike: Knitting
              Glass of water
Set: Two empty blood bottles

SCENE 4

Strike: Blood bottles

Off stage: Glass of water

SCENE 5

On stage: As before

SCENE 6

Set: Blood bottles
              Spilt blood

Off stage: Mirror (**Marianne**)

SCENE 7

Strike: Blood bottles
              Blood

Off stage: Keys (**Natalia**)

LIGHTING PLOT

ACT I, Scene 1

To open: Darkness

Cue 1	**Valentine** switches on the light *Bring up interior lighting on living-room area*	(Page 1)
Cue 2	**Valentine** leaves *Fade lights*	(Page 4)

ACT I, Scene 2

To open: Interior lighting on bathroom area

Cue 3	**Natalia**: "See you later, hypno boy." *Fade lights*	(Page 6)

ACT I, Scene 3

To open: Interior lighting on living-room area (Hayley's flat)

Cue 4	**Hayley** storms out *Black-out*	(Page 7)

ACT I, Scene 4

To open: Interior lighting on kitchen area (florist shop)

Cue 5	**Hayley**: "Bye." *Fade lights*	(Page 9)

ACT I, Scene 5

To open: Interior lighting on living-room area

Cue 6	**Valentine**: "Cool." *Black-out*	

ACT I, Scene 6

To open: Interior lighting on kitchen area (florist shop)

Cue 7	**Valentine** sneezes	(Page 12)
	Black-out	

ACT I, Scene 7

To open: Interior lighting on living-room area

Cue 8	**Natalia**: " ... we may have a problem."	(Page 15)
	Black-out	

ACT I, Scene 8

To open: Interior lighting on kitchen area (restaurant)

Cue 9	**Valentine**: " ... white should be fine."	(Page 16)
	Black-out	

ACT I, Scene 9

To open: Darkness

Cue 10	Sound of plane landing and flapping of wings	(Page 17)
	Bring up interior lighting on living-room area	

Cue 11	**Vincent** leaves	(Page 18)
	Black-out	

ACT I, Scene 10

To open: Interior lighting on kitchen area (restaurant)

Cue 12	**Hayley** and **Valentine** exit	(Page 19)
	Black-out	

ACT I, Scene 11

To open: Exterior lighting, street

Cue 13	**Hayley**: "Don't look now, but there's a cloud."	(Page 20)
	Black-out	

Lighting Plot

ACT I, Scene 12

To open: Interior lighting on living-room area

Cue 14	**Marianne**: "Yes, dear." *Black-out*	(Page 22)

ACT I, Scene 13

To open: Interior lighting on living-room area

Cue 15	**Natalia** goes over to **Valentine** and holds him *Black-out*	(Page 23)

ACT I, Scene 14

To open: Interior lighting on living-room area

Cue 16	**Natalia**: "... remember, no clinching!" *Black-out*	(Page 25)

ACT I, Scene 15

To open: Interior lighting on living-room area (Hayley's flat)

Cue 17	**Valentine**: "Nothing." *Black-out*	(Page 28)

ACT I, Scene 16

To open: Interior lighting on living-room area

Cue 18	**Valentine**: "Nothing." *Black-out*	(Page 28)
Cue 19	**Valentine** exits *Fade lights on one half of stage (bathroom area)*	(Page 30)
Cue 20	**Marianne** enters bathroom area *Bring up lights on bathroom area*	(Page 30)
Cue 21	**Valentine** begins to struggle *Fade lights to black on bathroom area*	(Page 32)
Cue 22	**Valentine** and **Natalia** move into kitchen area *Fade lights on living-room area and bring up on kitchen area*	(Page 33)

Cue 23   **Natalia**: "Oh not on account of me I hope."   (Page 34)
             Bring up interior lighting on living-room area

Cue 24   **Hayley**: "We really shouldn't do it again sometime."   (Page 34)

ACT I, SCENE 17

To open: Interior lighting on living-room area (Hayley's flat)

No cues

ACT I, SCENE 18

To open: Interior lighting on living-room area

Cue 25   **Natalia** exits   (Page 37)
             Fade lights

Cue 26   **Valentine** enters and hangs upside down   (Page 37)
             Bring up lights

Cue 27   **Valentine**: "No."   (Page 39)
             Black-out

ACT I, SCENE 19

To open: Interior lighting on living-room area (hotel room)

Cue 28   **Vincent**: "As is a vampire's hatred."   (Page 41)
             Fade lights to black-out

ACT I, SCENE 20

To open: Interior lighting on living-room area with curtains drawn

Cue 29   **Valentine** goes to remove **Hayley**'s top   (Page 42)
             Black-out

ACT II, SCENE 1

To open: Darkness

Cue 30   When ready   (Page 43)
             Bring up interior lighting on living-room area

Cue 31   **Hayley** and **Valentine** kiss   (Page 44)
             Fade lights to black

ACT II, Scene 2

To open: Darkness

Cue 32	**Hayley** switches the light on *Bring up interior lighting on kitchen area*	(Page 44)
Cue 33	**Valentine**: "Thank you." *Black-out*	(Page 46)

ACT II, Scene 3

To open: Interior lighting on kitchen area

Cue 34	**Natalia** hugs **Valentine** *Fade lights to black-out*	(Page 48)

ACT II, Scene 4

To open: Interior lighting on living-room area (Hayley's flat)

Cue 35	**Valentine**: "Goodbye, Hayley." *Black-out*	(Page 49)

ACT II, Scene 5

To open: Interior lighting on living-room area

Cue 36	**Valentine** and **Marianne** exit *Fade lights*	(Page 57)

ACT II, Scene 6

To open: Interior lighting on kitchen area

Cue 37	**Marianne** and **Hayley** exit *Fade lights*	(Page 64)

ACT II, Scene 7

To open: Interior lighting on kitchen area (the florist shop)

Cue 38	**Marianne**: "We all will." *Black-out*	(Page 66)

EFFECTS PLOT

ACT I

Cue 1   To open   (Page 1)
Sound of key turning in lock

Cue 2   To open SCENE 9   (Page 17)
Sound of plane landing and flapping of wings

Cue 3   **Marianne**: "... we leave." Long pause   (Page 30)
Transformation sound

Cue 4   **Valentine**: "... please no."   (Page 30)
Doorbell rings

Cue 5   **Marianne**: "What, why?"   (Page 30)
Doorbell rings again

Cue 6   **Natalia**: "... on regaining human form."   (Page 31)
Doorbell rings again

ACT II

Cue 7   Lights fade up   (Page 43)
Creepy music plays

Cue 8   **Valentine** walks around menancingly   (Page 44)
Music stops suddenly

Cue 9   **Marianne** exits. Pause   (Page 51)
Doorbell rings